what am I?

A Picture Book of Rhyming Christmas Riddles

WRITTEN BY SHANA GORIAN
ILLUSTRATED BY A. FYLYPENKO

What Am I? Christmas:
A Picture Book of Rhyming Christmas Riddles
Copyright © 2022 Shana Gorian. All rights reserved.

Written by Shana Gorian
Illustrated by A. Fylypenko aka. ArtPortra

First Edition, 2022

I dance and I prance
on my hoofs in thin air.
If you look to the sky,
you might see me up there.

what am I?

A reindeer.

I'm a helper, for sure,
and I work all year through.
I like to build toys
to be delivered to you.

what am I?

An elf.

I come in all shapes,
and I taste very sweet.
Open the oven door,
and let's bake a treat!

what am I?

A cookie.

I fly in my sleigh
with my jingling bells.
My four-legged team
carries toys for your shelves.

Who am I?

Santa Clause.

My wings are all white,
and I watch over you.
I wear a gold halo,
and I sing hallelu(jah)!

What am I?

An angel.

I hang from a mantel
all day and all night.
If your feet get cold,
wear me, you might.

what am I?

A stocking.

I clink, and I chime,
and I jangle and ding.
You can find me in a
church tower.
When I move, I ring.

what am I?

A bell.

I'm placed under the tree
while young children sleep.
My paper and bows
make you smile, not weep.

What am I?

Presents.

Send me by mail
to your loved ones far away.
I'll bring joy and fine greetings
to brighten their day.

what am I?

A Christmas card.

Sometimes I'm fake,
and sometimes I'm real.
My lights and my ornaments
hold quite an appeal.

what am I?

A Christmas tree.

I'm a stick with a curve, and I'm all red and white. But if you like peppermint, then lick. Don't bite.

what am I?

A candy cane.

I'm round, and I'm green,
and I hang from a door.
I prefer wearing ribbons
and pinecones and more.

what am I?

A wreath.

I'm a holiday song
That spreads joy
and good cheer,
with words about angels
or shepherds
or Santa's reindeer.

what am I?

A Christmas carol.

Dress my walls with candy
if your hands are quite steady.
But fall down, I will,
if my foundation's not ready.

what am I?

A gingerbread house.

Merry Christmas, I say,
To friends near and far.
Another riddle for you, though:
Where do you put the star?

On the top of the tree?
Yes, that star, I meant!
Now go write some Christmas cards.
They need to be sent!

There's only one more question
In this book of rhyme:
What season brings joy and high spirits?
Christmastime!

Shana Gorian is the author of the Rosco the Rascal series, early middle grade novels for kids ages 6-10. She loves holidays and seasons, and she loves to rhyme even when no one is listening.

Look for more seasonal, fun-loving books in the **What am I?** series for kids

A. Fylypenko is the artist behind the ARTPORTRA brand. Her extensive experience in illustration and design helps her breathe life into the unique concepts brought to her by creative clients from around the world.

Made in the USA
Las Vegas, NV
11 December 2024